Daniel Coit Gilman, America Project Making of

Statement of the progress and condition of the University of California : prepared by request of the Regents of the University

Daniel Coit Gilman, America Project Making of

Statement of the progress and condition of the University of California : prepared by request of the Regents of the University

ISBN/EAN: 9783337185176

Printed in Europe, USA, Canada, Australia, Japan

Cover: Foto ©Andreas Hilbeck / pixelio.de

More available books at **www.hansebooks.com**

STATEMENT

\

OF THE

PROGRESS AND CONDITION

OF THE

UNIVERSITY OF CALIFORNIA.

———— •◦•— ————

PREPARED BY REQUEST OF THE REGENTS OF THE UNIVERSITY,

BY DANIEL C. GILMAN, PRESIDENT., 1831 - 1908.

————— •◦•— —————

BERKELEY:
1875.

STATEMENT.

BERKELEY (NEAR OAKLAND), March 23d, 1875.

TO THE BOARD OF REGENTS, UNIVERSITY OF CALIFORNIA:

GENTLEMEN—In resigning the office of President of the University of California, I beg leave to submit a statement of the progress of the University during my connection with it.

1. The personal changes which have occurred during the past two years and a half are numerous.

My revered predecessor, Dr. Henry Durant, after a long life devoted to the public service, was removed by death January 22d, 1875. The tributes which have been paid to his character are already so ample, that here it is only necessary to place on record our grateful appreciation of his wisdom, his devotion, and his success in keeping alive the idea of a university in California, and in laboring for its foundation with untiring industry. It is a cause of regret that he has left behind him so little, in print or in manuscript, which will explain to those who come after him the peculiar difficulties and trials which he encountered. Some anecdotes noted down by a short-hand writer one evening at the request of a friend, as Dr. Durant related them, have been preserved in illustration of his experience, and his associates have told in various ways the story of his life; but his fame will depend on the place he has won in the roll of those who helped to found the institutions of California.

2. Hon. Edward Tompkins, a member of the Board of Regents and State Senator from Alameda County, died Novem-

2

ber 14th, 1872.. He had been one of the most constant and
efficient friends of the University, from the time of its organization, and the Regents placed on their records soon
after his death a full expression of their respect and grati-
tude.   Rev. Dr. Stebbins presented the following minute,
which was adopted by the Board:

"The Board of Regents hereby place on record their high appreciation of
the services and character of their late associate, the Honorable Edward
Tompkins, who, at the time of his death, was a State Senator for Alameda
County, and an elected member of this Board.

"He was a native of Oneida County, New York; a graduate of Union
College ; a successful member of the bar, first in his native State and then in
California ; a student of literary and philosophical subjects ; an earnest advo-
cate of the higher education, and the generous promoter of all good undertak-
ings in the community where he dwelt.

"He became a member of this Board in 1868, and served on the Committee
on Instruction. His residence in Oakland and the comparative leisure of his
late days enabled him to devote much time and thought to the internal affairs
of the University, and to present its claims with an intelligent appreciation of
details whenever there was occasion. Although suffering with an illness
which proved to be mortal, he came from a sick bed to preside and speak at
the inauguration of the President of the University on the 7th of November
last, and on the 14th of November, at the age of fifty-seven years, laid down
his life in the hope of the life to come.

"As the Public Orator of the University in many academic assemblies, as
the Counselor on whom the Academic Senate and the Board of Regents
were accustomed to rely, as the Legislator by whose persistent advocacy a
building fund was secured, and as a benefactor by whose munificence a professorship has been founded for instruction in Chinese and Japanese, he will
through all time be gratefully remembered in the annals of this University,
while his virtuous private life and his devotion to the public good deserve the
tribute of affectionate respect from all who were associated with him."   *

3. The presidency of the Board of Regents, which devolves
by law upon the Governor of the State, was transferred in
February, 1875, from Hon. Newton Booth (then U. S. Sena-
tor-elect), to Hon. Romualdo Pacheco (then Lieutenant-governor).

The office of Secretary, held by Mr. Andrew J. Moul-
der from an early period in the life of the University,
was given up by him in January, 1874. Its duties were
temporarily discharged by Mr. J. West Martin, one of the
Board of Regents, until April, 1874, when Mr. R. E. C.
Stearns was appointed to the place. The duties of this office

are exceedingly complex and difficult, and the University has been fortunate in having such incumbents of the post. Their devotion to the public welfare, their versatility, and their integrity have contributed largely to the prosperity of the institution.

The office of Land Agent was vacated by the death of the incumbent in 1874, and its duties were temporarily assigned to the Secretary, but there were serious difficulties in this arrangement, and it was given up. Mr. J. W. Shanklin was subsequently appointed Land Agent.

4. Among all the administrative offices of the Board, but one has remained unchanged: that of the Treasurer. The office has been filled from the beginning by W. C. Ralston, Esq., and to his energy and liberality the University is indebted for its good credit, and for the promptness with which its obligations are paid. Those who are familiar with new institutions elsewhere, of uncertain resources, can best appreciate the services of a treasurer so able and so willing.

5. The changes in the Board of Regents have been as follows, from November, 1872, to March, 1875:

RESIGNATIONS, ETC.

EDWARD TOMPKINS.............................Died Nov. 14th, 1872.
S. F. BUTTERWORTH............................Resigned.
RICHARD P. HAMMOND.........................Resigned.
CHARLES F. REED..............................Term expired.
T. B. SHANNON................................Term expired.
JOHN W. DWINELLE............................Resigned.
SAMUEL MERRITT..............................Resigned.
NEWTON BOOTH...............................Resigned as Governor.

ACCESSIONS TO OFFICE:

HENRY H. HAIGHT................By election of the Regents.
J. W. WINANS....................By appointment of the Governor.
R. S. CAREY.....................As Pres. State Agricultural Society.
M. M. ESTEE ....As Speaker of the Assembly.
D. C. GILMAN....................As President of the University.
J. M. HAMILTON ....By appointment of the Governor.
D. O. MILLS......................By appointment of the Governor.
WILLIAM MEEK...................By appointment of the Governor.
WILLIAM IRWIN..................As Lieutenant-Governor.

6. There have also been changes in the staff of teachers. The resignation of Professor Swinton, Professor of English

Literature and History, was accepted March 3d, 1874. He had previously requested a leave of absence, which had been refused by the Regents. His resignation was followed by the publication of a pamphlet in which his views on the subject of agricultural education were set forth.

The resignation of Dr. E. S. Carr, Professor of Agriculture, was requested by the Regents in July, 1874, and when the request was not complied with, he was removed from office for reasons which were briefly stated. He also published a pamphlet containing animadversions on the action of the Regents, and particularly in respect to their management of the "Agricultural Department." His removal caused a remonstrance on the part of the "Patrons of Husbandry," or Grangers, and the "Mechanics' Deliberative Assembly," which was answered by the Board of Regents in a brief communication.

7. In the summer of 1873, Professor Samuel Jones, Professor of Military Science, etc., was called away to become President of the Maryland College of Agriculture. His resignation was accepted with reluctance, and the thanks of the Board of Regents were formally voted to him for his able and efficient services.

Two instructors of modern languages, Mr. Julius Grossman and Mr. Manuel M. Corella, have also resigned, the latter having finished a course of special studies in the University and returned to Mexico.

8. The vacancies thus created have all been filled, and there have been other important additions to the corps of instructors. The names and departments of instruction of those who have been appointed since November, 1872, are as follows :   ·

PROFESSORS.

Agriculture...............................EUGENE W. HILGARD.
Mining...................................WILLIAM ASHBURNER.
Industrial Mechanics......................FREDERICK G. HESSE.
English...................................EDWARD R. SILL.
Military Science, etc......................SAMUEL JONES.

LECTURERS.

Metallurgy ....GEORGE F. BECKER.
Economic Botany..........................C. E. BESSEY.
Stock Breeding...........................WILLIAM H. BREWER.

Industrial Drawing........................JOHN D. HOFFMANN.
Spanish ....CHARLES F. GOMPERTZ.
German ....ALBIN PUTZKER.
French....................................G. DE KERSAINT-GILY.

ASSISTANTS.

Mathematics..............................GEORGE C. EDWARDS.
Mathematics ....LEANDER L. HAWKINS.
Classics ....ARTHUR H. ALLEN.
Classics ....AMBROSE C. RICHARDSON.
Chemistry................................F. SLATE, JR.
Chemistry ....JOHN D. STILLMAN.
Chemistry ....SAMUEL B. CHRISTY.
Mineralogy ....A. WENDELL JACKSON.
English ....JOSEPH C. ROWELL.
English..................................THOMAS F. BARRY.
Mechanics................................EDWARD A. PARKER.

OTHER OFFICERS.

Superintendent of the Grounds.............R. E. C. STEARNS.
Landscape Engineer.......................W. HAMMOND HALL.
Gardener.................................JOHN ELLIS.
Curator of the Mineralogical Collections, etc.HENRY G. HANKS.
Foreman of the Printing Office............A. WHITTON.
Student Manager ....L. A. JORDAN.

9. The Chair of Agriculture has been filled by the appointment of Professor Eugene W. Hilgard, Ph. D., formerly of the College of Agriculture and Mechanic Arts in the University of Mississippi, and recently of the University of Michigan. While in Mississippi he had charge of the Geological and Agricultural Survey of the State. Mr. Hilgard's eminence as a man of science, his skill in applying his knowledge to agriculture and other industrial pursuits, and his long experience as a teacher, have qualified him in an uncommon degree to discharge with satisfaction the difficult duties devolved upon him. He is well known for the attention which he has given to the analysis of soils, and for the light he has thus thrown upon some of the most intricate problems in agricultural science. He came to Berkeley in the autumn of 1874, and delivered there two courses of lectures; one upon the General Principles of Agriculture (particularly upon the chemistry of soils) and the other on the Chemistry

of Household Life. The impression which he made by these lectures was so good that he was unanimously appointed permanent professor, and he is now about to enter upon his duties among us.

10. The Chair of Mining has been filled by the appointment of Mr. William Ashburner, mining engineer, of San Francisco, who will direct his attention to the organization of the College of Mines, as fast as the funds are provided for this purpose. Mr. Ashburner, having received a technical and scientific education in the East and in Europe, came early to the Pacific Coast, and was for a time engaged upon the Geological Survey of California. He has had ample opportunities for becoming acquainted with the mining industries of this and other countries, and he has already made his influence felt for good upon the students of this University. In entering upon his professorship, he delivered an introductory lecture on the Profession of Mining Engineering, which has been printed.

11. A Chair of Industrial Mechanics was instituted by the Board in the autumn of 1874, and was subsequently filled by the appointment of Mr. Frederick G. Hesse, of Oakland. Mr. Hesse was trained in a German polytechnic school, and was early engaged as a teacher in Brown University. He subsequently held a scientific appointment under the United States Government, but has resided for the last few years in Oakland, engaged in mechanical occupations, especially in the invention and improvement of some ingenious mechanical contrivances. It is rare to find a man qualified to fill the duties of a Chair of Industrial Mechanics, both by his scientific attainments, and by practical knowledge acquired in the shop, but Mr. Hesse is such a man. Upon assuming the duties of his post, he delivered a lecture on the Profession of Mechanical Engineering, which will be printed. He is now engaged in devising implements by which a thorough examination may be made of the strength of the timbers of the Pacific Coast, to which reference will be made in a later portion of this report.

12. The professorship of English was filled by the ap-

pointment of Mr. Edward R. Sill, a graduate of Yale College, who has been engaged in teaching in California for several years, and is highly esteemed for his literary attainments, for his enthusiasm in the study of language, and for his devotion to the work of a teacher. His introductory lecture on the subject of the Study of English was printed in the *Berkeleyan.*

13. The vacancy occasioned by the withdrawal of Professor Jones was filled by the appointment of two graduates of the University to be assistants in mathematics—Mr. George C. Edwards and Mr. Leander L. Hawkins—and they have during the last two years discharged this service with great fidelity. Mr. Edwards has had the command of the battalion in addition to his duties as mathematical instructor, and Mr. Hawkins has had the chief direction of the classes in surveying.

14. Mr. John D. Hoffmann was appointed in the autumn of 1874 instructor of Industrial Drawing. He is an experienced engineer and draughtsman, who was trained in Germany, has had long experience in the construction of public works, especially in the service of the U. S. Government, and he is in all respects qualified to impart an exact knowledge of this most important art.

15. Mr. Albin Putzker entered upon his duties as special instructor in German, in the spring of 1874, and has succeeded in a remarkable degree in awakening a love of the study of that language among all classes of students. He was previously head of the Santa Barbara College.

16. The large number of scholars pursuing the study of French, under Professor Pioda, made it indispensable to provide an additional instructor in that department, and Mr. G. de Kersaint-Gily has accordingly been appointed. The place occupied by Mr. Corella as instructor in Spanish has been filled by the appointment of Mr. Charles D. Gompertz, who also devotes much attention to the Library.

17. Mr. Arthur H. Allen, graduate of Yale College, who was employed for a single year as instructor in the College of Letters, discharged these duties with skill and success until

he was released from service at his own request. The place
he had held was filled by the appointment of Mr. A. C. Richardson, a graduate of Harvard College, distinguished for his
knowledge of the classics, who still continues to give instruction.

18. In the summer of 1874, the Regents determined to appoint as assistant instructors several young men who had recently graduated. The amount of their compensation was not
to be large ($600 per year), and it was not supposed that their
duties would be responsible or onerous. But it was thought
that they would be led to prosecute advanced studies under
the direction of the Faculty, and would thus become better
fitted for the duties of life. This plan, which is nearly
equivalent to the establishment of graduate scholarships, has
worked well. Two of this company of young men have been
granted leave of absence without pay for one year, to pursue
their studies in Germany ; four others are to remain a
second year ; the seventh begins a professional course of
study in law. The names of these seven graduate students
are as follows: T. F. Barry, S. B. Christy, A. W. Jackson,
E. A. Parker, J. C. Rowell, F. Slate, J. M. Stillman.

19. Professor George Davidson, a non-resident professor,
who began to give instruction in Geodesy and the use of astronomical instruments in the winter of 1873, was inter-
rupted in this work by being called upon to engage in the
observations of the transit of Venus, in Japan.

20. Hon. S. J. Field, non-resident Professor of Law, proposes to commence a course of lectures in the Spring of
1875.

21. The staff giving instructions at Berkeley now includes
the President, thirteen resident Professors, two non-resident Professors (Judge Field and Prof. Davidson), three
lecturers for the current year (Professors Bessey and Brewer,
and Dr. Becker), nine instructors, and seven graduate assistants. There, are in addition, a Superintendent of the Agricultural Grounds, a Gardener, a Foreman and a Manager of the
Printing Office, and there are also occasional lecturers,
whose services have been gratuitously given on one or more
days.

22. The number of students has steadily increased since the opening of the institution, as the following figures show:

In 1869–70.. 40
In 1870–71.. 78
In 1871–72...153
In 1872–73...185
In 1873–74...191
In 1874–75...234

The inconveniences at Berkeley were so many when the University was first established in its permanent place, that many of those who had proposed to enter were prevented from doing so, and some of the ladies who had been in attendance withdrew from the classes. Since the close of the last academic year, 126 persons have applied for admission to the University. Twenty-six counties of this State, and several states of the Union, have their representatives at Berkeley. Of the present students, 171 are candidates for a degree. The number of ladies attending the classes is thirty-nine. There is no preparatory class.

LEGISLATION.

23. In entering upon the office which I have held, it was my first duty to become acquainted with the laws under which the University was organized, with the policy that the Regents had adopted for the organization of the University, and with the requirements of the community in respect to higher education. It was soon apparent that a great diversity of views prevailed in respect to the scope of the University, and that these difficulties arose in part from the varied enactments under which the institution had been organized. A few words upon this subject may tend, perhaps, both to exhibit and to remove some of these difficulties.

24. The State of California, like most of the newer States of the Union, received from the General Government a certain portion of the public lands for the use of a seminary of learning; and the Constitution of the State provided for the bestowal of these and other funds upon a State University. This was the nucleus of the University of California.

25. Independent of State action, a private corporation, established in Oakland, maintained for several years an institution of learning under the name of the College of California. It acquired lands, funds, and good-will. When the University was organized it relinquished the field and gave up its property to the State, on condition of the perpetual maintenance of a College of Letters.

26. In 1862, the National Government bestowed on the various States of the Union a certain amount of scrip in the public lands, for the maintenance in each State of "at least one college where the leading object shall be, without excluding other scientific and classical studies, and including military tactics, to teach such branches of learning as are related to agriculture and the mechanical arts, in such manner as the legislatures of the States may respectively prescribe, in order to promote the liberal and practical education of the industrial classes in the several pursuits and professions in life."

27. The scope of this national endowment has been well defined by many writers, but by none more clearly than in the following paragraph, which was written by Professor Atherton, once of the Illinois Industrial University, and now of the Rutgers Scientific School in New Brunswick, New Jersey. After referring to the terms of the grant as prescribed by Congress, he says:

"This language certainly does not contemplate the teaching of "agriculture" alone, but of all the natural sciences which underlie its laws and processes, all the mathematical and physical sciences which are the basis of the mechanic arts, and whatever else is adapted to promote "the liberal and practical education of the industrial classes," not even excluding classical studies. It is, in short, the statement of a comprehensive scheme for promoting the higher education of the people—a thing which the Government has been doing ever since it first had public lands to dispose of. The institutions thus founded have come to be generally spoken of as "agricultural colleges," simply for want of a more convenient designation, and probably, also, because "agriculture" happens to be the first important word in that part of the law just quoted."

28. After prolonged discussion among the friends of higher education, the Legislature organized the University of Cali-

fornia by an Act approved March 23d, 1868, which was somewhat modified by the passage of the Political Code, and has since received some additional amendments. The "Organic Act," thus modified, still governs the University. It is printed with the last legislative revisions in the University Registers for 1874 and 1875.

29. The Board of Regents, on whom these laws devolved the administration of the University, was originally constituted as follows, in four distinct classes:

a. The Governor, Lieutenant Governor, and State Superintendent of Schools, all elected by popular vote, and holding office for four years, and the Speaker of the Assembly, holding office for two years, and elected by members of the Assembly, were the official representatives of the State.

b. The President of the State Agricultural Society and the President of the Mechanics' Institute in San Francisco, elected annually by these societies, were the representatives of the agricultural and mechanical interests of the State.

c. Eight members of the Board, holding office for sixteen years, were appointed by the Governor, with the approval of the Senate.

d. Eight members of the Board, holding office for sixteen years, were elected as honorary Regents, and were chosen "from the body of the State by the official and appointed members."

30. The law expressly declared that no member of the Board should be deemed a public officer by virtue of such membership; but he should be deemed as discharging exclusively a private trust. The Regents were furthermore required to become incorporated under the general laws of the State. These provisions were intended to secure stability in the Board, and the removal of the University from political interference; while at the same time the official representatives of the State had power to prevent and correct abuses. Care was also taken, by providing six different modes of membership, and tenures of office which vary in length from one to sixteen years, that the Board should not be the representative of any class or faction.

Sectarian and ecclesiastical influences were precluded by a requirement that a majority of the Board should not be "of any one religious sect, or of no religious sect."

31. The Political Code of the State of California, which went into operation on the 1st of January, 1873, made sev-

eral changes in the constitution of the Board of Regents, the bearing of which upon the management of the University does not seem to have been fully considered. The Regents are declared to be civil executive officers of the State, and all except the *ex officio* members are to be appointed, as vacancies occur, by the Governor, with the advice and consent of the Senate.

By the Legislature of 1873–4, the President of the University for the time being was made a member of the Board, and some slight verbal changes were made in the law.

This is not the place to suggest further changes in the Organic Act, but some changes must be made before the University can be regarded as established on a sure foundation.

32. It would be well for the State if these historic statements in respect to the origin of the University of California were more generally remembered. It is frequently asserted that the University was founded as an Agricultural College, and that the College of Letters should have no place in the organization; whereas the truth is, that the State, in its Constitution, provided for the establishment of "a University," and all subsequent legislation has tended toward a liberal and comprehensive institution in which all higher studies should be taught.

ADMINISTRATION.

33. Many changes have been made in the mode of conducting the business of the Board—one of the most important of which has been the establishment of the Secretary's office at the site of the University, where he can personally oversee the expenditures of money. Another noteworthy change has been made in the organization of the committees of the Board.

The number of standing committees was originally twelve. This plan had doubtless been adopted in order to interest every member of the Board in some department of the University's service, but the practical working of the arrangement had been to diffuse responsibility and to lessen interest. Recognizing this fact, the Board, at my request, soon determined to appoint one committee which should be a central committee and should be advisory to the President in the discharge of his duties. This committee was appointed by ballot, and consisted of five members, three of whom were to be residents of Alameda County. The members of this committee were originally Messrs. H. H. Haight, S. F. Butterworth, H. Stebbins, J. W. Dwinelle, and J. W. Martin. The place of Mr. Butterworth was subsequently filled by the appointment of Mr. J. Mora Moss. This committee has met frequently at the call of one of their number or of the President, and has devoted a very large amount of time to the consideration of all the affairs of the University. No important steps have been taken by the President without their knowledge and consent, and on them the Board of Regents has relied for advice in matters pertaining to the instruction and government of the students and the appointment of instructors. Their meetings have been held on an average more frequently than once a month and have often been prolonged for two or three hours. The visits of the various members of the Committee to Berkeley have likewise been frequent.

As a still further step toward efficient administration, the Board determined to make the quarterly meeting of June an annual meeting, and to require at that time the presentation of reports respecting the various departments of the University and the discussion of the most important measures, so far as they could be foreseen, for the ensuing year. The annual meeting for 1874 was held at Berkeley in the month of June.

The number of the Committees has been reduced from twelve to five, and their duties are as follows:

1. The Advisory Committee, to advise the Board and the President on all such matters as may be referred to them.

2. The Finance Committee, to audit all bills and to supervise the financial affairs of the University.

3. The Land Committee, to supervise the work of the Land Agent, and to superintend the sale of the national land grant.

4. The Committee on Buildings and Grounds, to supervise the care of the property of the University.

5. The Law Committee, to give advice on legal points.

SURVEYS OF THE SITE.

34. The right development of a site which is to be the seat of a University for a long time to come has naturally required a great deal of consideration, and much of this preliminary work has been done since 1872.

35. The College of California, before it transferred the Berkeley property to the University, had caused it to be carefully examined by the well-known landscape engineer of New York, Mr. Frederick Law Olmsted, who prepared a plan for its improvement, accompanied by an elaborate map. The date of his report was June 29th, 1866. His views in respect to the uses of the grounds were published in a pamphlet, and are still of much value; but the organization of the institution, when it passed from the control of a private corporation to that of the State, was varied, and this made it necessary to deviate in many respects from his suggestions. It is obvious that the requirements of a State University were very different from those of a simple college.

Copies of Mr. Olmsted's report are now scarce, and it would be well if such portions as are of permanent value could be reprinted. All my endeavours to find the map which Mr. Olmsted prepared have been without success. When the Regents of the University entered upon the site, Mr. Low, a landscape gardener of San José, was employed to lay out the roads and paths which were most requisite. It became important also to determine upon the bearings which should be given to the college buildings which were first to be constructed. It was decided by the architect to place them at right angles to an axial line which divides the property into two nearly equal portions, and which protracted bisects the Golden Gate.

36. As a trustworthy basis for future improvements, the

Regents requested the Chief of the United States Coast Survey work on the Pacific to cause a plane-table survey of the site to be made. This was done in the spring of 1873 by Mr. Cleveland Rockwell.

At a later day, Mr. William Hammond Hall, the Landscape Engineer of the Golden Gate Park of San Francisco, was requested by the Regents to present a plan for the improvement of the grounds, having in view what had already been done, and what were likely to be the requirements of the University during a long period to come. His plan, which is dated February 21st, 1874, is printed in the statement of the Regents to the Legislature in the session of 1873–4. It has been approved and adopted by the Board.

An accurate survey of the boundary lines has also been made.

There are now no funds for the general improvement of the grounds, as the resources set apart for out-of-door work are devoted to the development of the agricultural and horticultural department. As soon as the means of the University permit, the work of road-making and grading should be prosecuted with efficiency.

37. In further preparation for the growth of the University, the students of Civil Engineering, under the guidance of the professor in that department, are making a very minute survey of the site.

Two parts of this survey have been completed, the region around the two large buildings now constructed, and the water-shed and water-courses connected with the water supply of the University.

Professor Soulé has made an elaborate report, which remains in manuscript, upon the water question, having in view not only the present necessities of the institution, but also the probability that a large neighborhood will require to be supplied from the springs which the University controls. This report might well be printed. He has also furnished the following note in respect to the topography of the site:

" I have found already in my teaching that the topography of the site is not only beautiful in a landscape and architectural point of view, but is excellently adapted to instruction in all branches of field engineering. The diversified character of the surface brings into use all the systems and principles of surveying and topography. It is in area 200 acres, is watered by numerous springs in the hills, and the collection and disposal of this will furnish hereafter abundant study and practice to the engineering student. With the spring water and surface water saved, the grounds could be thoroughly irrigated throughout the year, and made to blossom as the rose. The lower portion of the grounds is flat and moist throughout the year, and will nourish such trees, flowers, and shrubs, as require such soil. Then there is a higher plateau, upon which the various buildings have been, or are to be located, forming the *campus* proper. Beyond, toward the Monte Diablo Range, the ground rises into hills, the highest of which is 884 feet above tide-water, and 584 feet above the base of the south college. The average height of the tract is 400 feet above tide-water. The hilly portion could be well utilized for forestry. The University is supplied with water from a reservoir of 38,000 gallons capacity, situated at the foot of Strawberry Cañon, and at an elevation of 205 feet above the basement of the south college. It will carry water entirely over any building contemplated. Other springs of large resources will be reclaimed and brought in, from time to time. Strawberry Creek is for a large portion of the year a beautifully clear stream; during the winter it discharges an enormous quantity of water, and runs between steep banks ten to fifteen feet in depth, and with a span from thirty to 100 feet. Along it are found many shady quiet nooks, gracious to the scholar, philosopher, and naturalist. The soil of the lower portion of the site is a deep, rich adobe, capable of being wrought into a soil of great productiveness; on the plateau it is a lighter kind. On the hills there is a thin soil of decomposed shale rock, etc. It would be difficult to find within so small an area as the University site a spot with so many varieties and capabilities in the way of soils, irrigation, and exposure."

38. The University has thus at command several accurate maps of its Berkeley property, viz:

a. The plane-table map prepared by Mr. Rockwell, of the U. S. Coast Survey.

b. The project for the improvement of the grounds, by Mr. W. H. Hall, of San Francisco.

c. The survey of the boundary lines.

d. The survey of the water rights of the University and their connections, prepared by Professor Soulé.

e. Detailed plats of different portions of the grounds, prepared by the students in Engineering and Surveying. Mr. Hawkins has taken special interest in the study of the site, and in ascertaining accurate data in respect to its characteristics.

BUILDINGS.

39. Two large and commodious buildings have been constructed for the University at Berkeley. The plans for these structures were made by Mr. David Farquharson, architect, of San Francisco, and were adopted by the Board before my connection with the University. The brick building sometimes called the College of Agriculture, but officially designated by the Regents as the "South Hall," was constructed under the direction of Mr. Farquharson; the wooden building, sometimes called the College of Letters, but officially designated as the "North Hall," was constructed without the architect's supervision, and the interior arrangements were in some respects changed from his original plans by the direction of the Board of Regents. The corner-stone of the first building was laid in August, 1872, with public ceremonies; the corner-stone of the second building was laid in the spring of 1873, in the presence of the officers and students of the University.

Both these buildings were occupied at the commencement of the college year in September, 1873, although some of the interior arrangements were not completed.

The South Hall contains the Library, museums, laboratories, Agricultural rooms, Secretary's office, and an admirable scientific lecture-room. The North Hall contains the class-rooms for Mathematics, Physics, Engineering, Mechanics, Languages, and Literature, together with a large assembly-room, Faculty rooms, armory, printing-office, etc.

The dimensions of the brick building are as follow: length, one hundred and fifty-two feet; average width, fifty-six feet. There are four stories, and thirty-four rooms in the building, six of them being thirty-two by forty-eight feet, and several of the others twenty by twenty-six feet.

The length of the north building is one hundred and sixty-six feet; its average width, sixty feet, and its height sixty-four feet. It has four stories, and is divided into twenty-eight compartments. The assembly-room is forty-three by

3

fifty-eight feet, and the philosophical lecture room thirty-six by fifty-eight feet.

COURSES OF INSTRUCTION.

40. The changes in the courses of instruction during the last three years are partly such as have been occasioned by the increase in the number of teachers, and by the improved facilities for instruction afforded by the new buildings at Berkeley.

Some of these changes are important enough to be explained.

In addition to the original courses of study in Agriculture and Letters which were commenced in 1869, a course in Engineering was begun in 1871. Since then the courses in Mechanics, Mining, and Chemistry have been established, and the course in Letters has been separated into a classical and a literary course. In accordance with the phraseology of the laws of the State, these courses are commonly spoken of as " colleges." At the head of each of these seven departments of instruction is a professor, who acts under the President and Faculty as the director of the studies of the course.

These seven courses and their directors are as follows :

Agriculture .... PROFESSOR HILGARD.
Mechanics ....   "   JOHN LECONTE.
Mining..................................   "   ASHBURNER.
Chemistry ....   "   RISING.
Engineering ....   "   SOULE.
Classics................................   "   KELLOGG.
Literature..............................   "   SILL.

41. The five courses first named are commonly spoken of as the " College of Science," and the two last named as the " College of Letters." The Scientific Faculty and the Literary Faculty meet together as one body for the government of the students. All the Faculties of the University, including the Medical, constitute by law an " Academic Senate," the meetings of which will not probably be fre-

quent. The President of the University is the presiding officer in these various Faculties, and the Dean of·the Academic Senate is the Secretary of that body and of the joint meetings of the Scientific and Literary Faculties.

In the five technical courses, the first two years are devoted chiefly to those studies which are fundamental and of general importance—to Mathematics, Elementary Chemistry, Physics, Natural History, and Modern Languages, including English. During the last two years, the special subjects of the several courses predominate, that is to say, Agriculture, Mechanics, Mining, Chemistry, or Engineering. The degree given at the conclusion of each of these courses is that of Bachelor of Philosophy in the College of Agriculture, Mechanics, etc., as the case may be. Full particulars in regard to these courses are given in the Register of the University for 1874–5.

42. The examinations for admissions have been made more strict, but the terms of entrance have not been altered. To explain the character of these examinations, both to teachers and scholars in distant parts of the State, a circular has been carefully prepared and widely distributed. It is printed as Bulletin No. 6.

At the examinations for admission in the autumn of 1874, there were 126 candidates, of whom 54 were admitted without a condition, six withdrew of their own accord, and fifteen were found deficient in two principal studies and advised to withdraw. Of those who were admitted on condition of making up their deficiencies, nineteen were conditioned in mathematics, and in the College of Letters thirteen were conditioned in Latin.

There are two principal examinations every year, one at the end of the first term called the "semi-annual," and one at the end of the year called the "annual." These examinations cover the work which has been· done during the semester or the year just previous. The effect of these examinations on the standing of a scholar is carefully adjusted by rules which the Faculty have adopted.

43. The order of the University, during the three years, has been good. The number of cases requiring discipline from the Faculty for improper conduct has been exceedingly small. There has been no system of police, nor of tutorial or military supervision. There have been few regulations, and few penalties, but the constant effort of the instructors has been to impress upon the scholars a sense of the advantages here bestowed upon them, and to let it be understood that those who do not appreciate these advantages are liable at any moment to be deprived of them. This simple understanding has been sufficient to secure the respectful obedience of the pupils, and cases of neglect and carelessness have been exceedingly rare. Visitors to the public buildings are constantly surprised to see the good order in which they have been kept, and are more surprised to learn that this good condition is not the result of frequent repairs, nor of heavy penalties, but of constant attention and care on the part of the students.

TECHNICAL AND SCIENTIFIC INSTRUCTION.

44. From what has been already said, it is obvious that special attention has been given to technical or scientific instruction, in accordance with the terms of the Congressional grant, making it necessary to provide instruction in those branches of learning " which are related to Agriculture and Mechanical Arts." Five of these modern courses or colleges are now maintained in the University, namely:

1. Agriculture.   4. Engineering.
2. Mechanics.   5. Chemistry.
3. Mining.

45. The general character of this instruction is indicated by the following report from the Faculty, presented to the Legislative Committee, February 28th, 1874. Since that time the three deficiencies referred to at the close of their report have been supplied. First, the out-door work has been begun, including the establishment on a good plan of an orchard, botanic garden, propagating-houses, and experi-

ment station in agriculture and horticulture; second, instruction has been given by Professors Bessey and Brewer in economic Botany and Zoology; and third, special instructors have been appointed in Industrial Mechanics and Industrial Drawing.

"What is the course of study in the University of California, in Agriculture and Mechanic Arts?

"The Faculty of the University, February 28th, 1874, in reply to this formal inquiry, made the following answer. By a comparison of their statements with those of other kindred universities, it will be seen that the statement of Professor Carr is corroborated when he said to the Joint University Committee that with one special provision made, 'we shall compare very favorably with any agricultural college in the country so far as in-door instruction is concerned :'

"REPORT.—It may be premised that the object of the course of instruction given in the University in all its departments, including those of Agriculture and Mechanic Arts, is to furnish a broad and liberal culture adapted to the various callings of intelligent and educated citizens. With this aim in view, the course of instruction in the Colleges of Agriculture and Mechanic Arts has been so arranged as to embrace the following subjects:

"1. *An English Course:* embracing the history and structure of the English Language; Ancient and Modern History, Rhetoric, and Logic. This course extends through four years.

"2. A course in *Modern Languages:* embracing one or more modern languages, extending through three or four years.

"3. A complete course of *Mathematics,* as constituting the basis of all scientific education, extending through three years.

"4. A three.years' course of *Mechanics and Physics :* Mechanics, embracing the principles of machinery and the manifold applications of power, Hydrostatics, Hydraulics, and Pneumatics; Physics, embracing the principles of Heat and its various effects in Evaporation, Rain and Dew, etc.; the principles of the Steam-engine; Electricity, Magnetism, and Electro-magnetism; Acoustics, Optics, and other physical subjects, the knowledge of which is necessary to the intelligent farmer and mechanic.

"5. A three years' course in *Natural History and Geology.* The course in *Botany* embraces the Structure and Physiology of Plants—i. e., how plants germinate and grow and feed—the nature of their food, the circulation of sap, the changes which it undergoes, etc. The connection of this course with Agriculture is close and direct.

"The course in *Zoology* embraces Comparative Anatomy and Physiology, and the Laws of Reproduction in Animals. The connection of these subjects with stock-feeding and stock-breeding is evident.

"The relation of Geology to Agriculture is scarcely less important, since soils are derived from the disintegration of rocks, and their nature and fertility are, therefore, largely determined by the character of the country rock.

"6. A course of *Chemistry*, general and analytical, embracing qualitative and quantitative analysis and laboratory work. The importance of this course, as forming the basis of scientific agriculture and many branches of arts, is evident. This extends from two to four years.

"7. A course of *Engineering and Surveying*, which is important in its applications to irrigation and reclamation of lands.

"8. Courses in Astronomy, Physical Geography, and Political Economy.

"9. Besides these eight courses, which provide such a liberal culture as every educated citizen should possess, and many portions of which have a close connection with practical agriculture and mechanical arts, a *special course* is given to the students in the *Agricultural College*, by the Professor of Agriculture, on the subjects relating more specifically to that department.

"No special instruction is given in Applied Mechanics, except such as is given in the course of Mechanics and Physics, as no instructor has been provided for this department.

"The special instruction in Agriculture and Mechanic Arts is still deficient in desirable completeness. To meet this deficiency, the following suggestions are made:

"1. Facilities for scientific and practical experiments in *Agriculture* and *Horticulture*, including a Botanic Garden and an Arboretum.

"2. Instruction in *Economic Botany and Zoology*, including the study of insects injurious to vegetation, as recommended in the reports of the Regents.

"3. Special instruction in Applied Mechanics, as already recommended in the report of the Regents for 1873, pp. 29 and 30."

COLLEGE OF AGRICULTURE.

46. The most noteworthy changes in the College of Agriculture are the appointment of a new professor in that department, the commencement of field and garden work, and the enlistment of special lecturers to supplement the regular instructions of the professor.

The out-door work is subordinate and auxiliary to the class-room instructions of the Professor of Agriculture, but its general direction is intrusted by law to the Secretary. Under him an accomplished and experienced gardener has been employed.

47. On the 1st of February, 1875, Secretary Stearns made the following report of the work which he had commenced. A more extended statement may be expected before the session of the Legislature :

"On the first day of June, 1874, work in this department was commenced, and has been pursued with energy.

" A portion of the grounds dedicated to practical agriculture has been thoroughly plowed, graded, and otherwise prepared by deep trenching and working over, for nursery purposes.

"Two propagating-houses have been constructed and were ready for use in the latter part of August, 1874, and a commodious and convenient building for work-rooms, with suitable benches for potting and handling plants constructed, with storage arrangements for prepared soil, pots, tools, etc., and a suitable office for gardener, and sleeping-room for watchman.

"The propagating-houses are of the dimensions respectively of thirty by twenty feet, and sixty-four by fifteen feet, and in the rear of the latter is a laboratory pertaining to said houses, sixty-four feet in length by twelve feet in width; these buildings are arranged so as to facilitate the work, and so conveniently placed that the whole is easily supervised by the gardener.

" The propagation of plants of economic value, as well as such species as are more particularly required for the purpose of illustrating general botany, and ornamenting the grounds, in pursuance of the general plan devised by Mr. W. H. Hall, was at once commenced, and such vegetable forms as are valuable to the pomologist, and necessary to illustrate floriculture and arboriculture, have already been produced in large numbers. The entire domain belonging to the University includes two hundred acres, sloping to the west, a parallelogram in general shape, and presenting quite a diversified topography; its lower portion being about two hundred feet above the level of San Francisco Bay, and rising toward the east into hills, the summits of which are about nine hundred feet above the sea-level. Some forty acres are reserved for agricultural purposes and experiments, and the remainder to illustrate the principles and methods of landscape ornamentation, forestry, botany and allied studies.

" A well-designed and convenient barn, thirty-six by forty-four feet, and a story and a half in height, has been built, and the principal road which traverses the farming-grounds has been marked out and partly graded, to facilitate the farm work.

"The propagating-houses were ready for use on the 22d day of August, since which date 10,000 plants of 20 species of eucalyptus, 5,000 acacias of 25 species, 200 species of native and foreign coniferæ, also numerous rare forms peculiar to Australasia, South and Central America, and elsewhere, and many species of textile, medicinal, and other economic plants, have been produced. We may mention 112 varieties of roses, 13 of azaleas, 12 of camelias, and six of magnolias, for ornamental purposes.

" The planting of a standard orchard, for the purpose of correcting the nomenclature of the fruits already in cultivation, and for furnishing hereafter cions and plants for distribution through the State, as well as for the introduction of new varieties to be distributed as above, has received proper consideration. The following have already been planted, and it is our intention to still further enlarge the list:

Apples	141	varieties.
Siberian Crab-apples	14	"
Pears	152	"
Cherries	82	"
Plums	57	"
Peaches	89	"
Apricots	22	"
Quinces	2	"
Nectarines	15	"
Grapes	73	"
Blackberries	7	"
Gooseberries	8	"
Currants	8	"
Raspberries	34	"
Strawberries	35	"
Filberts	3	"
Asparagus	1	"
Rhubarb	16	"
Mulberries	6	"

And all the species of walnuts and chestnuts. We have also procured many varieties of oranges, lemons, limes, etc.

"Among the apples are nine new Russian varieties, and the peaches include seventeen of Rivers' new seedlings.

"Our thanks are due to many friends for plants and seeds of desirable varieties, both of ornamental and useful plants; especially so to Mr. Regent Bolander, Mr. S. Nolan, Dr. A. Kellogg, Mr. W. J. Fisher (Naturalist of the Tuscarora Telegraph Sounding Expedition); and to Dr. C. L. Anderson, of Santa Cruz, Cal., for choice species of willows, as well as to other parties who have presented smaller lots.

"It is not to be expected, with our local climate and soil, that all of the above can be successfully grown at Berkeley, but it is altogether probable that many of them can be successfully cultivated, and we may be able to add more or less to the number of useful varieties now produced in the State."

48. The gardener has utilized, so far as he could, the voluntary labor of some of the students, paying for it a fair price—the same as is paid to other working persons of like capacity. Those students who are especially enrolled in the College of Agriculture have had the opportunity of becoming acquainted with these out-of-door operations, and were required at the end of the first half-year to make reports upon the same.

The out-door work may be considered partly as agricultural, partly as horticultural, partly as botanical, or it may be regarded as having reference in part to the beautifying of the grounds, by planting upon them rare, useful, and ornamental trees, shrubs, flowers, etc., both native and exotic; and in part as having reference to the trial of experiments in the practical work of the farm or garden.

49. During the present college year, three distinguished lecturers from other colleges in which technical instruction is made prominent have given courses of lectures at Berkeley, and a miscellaneous course of lectures on agricultural subjects, by residents of California, has also been arranged. These lectures are given before the College of Agriculture, but are open to all persons who desire to attend them, whether members of the University or not.

At a future time, other courses of lectures may be expected; among them, a course by W. S. Clark, LL. D., President of the Massachusetts Agricultural College, Amherst, and a course by Professor E. S. Morse, A. M., of the Peabody Institute, Salem, Mass.

The lecturers and their subjects, for 1875, are as follow:

"1. On the Analysis of Soils: by Professor Eugene W. Hilgard, Ph. Dr. of the University of Michigan.

"2. On the Chemistry of Household Life: by Professor Eugene W. Hilgard, Ph. Dr., of the University of Michigan.

"3. On Economic Botany; or the Plants which are Useful and Harmful in Human Industry: by Professor C. E. Bessey, M. S., of the Iowa Agricultural College.

"4. On the Improvement of Varieties in Plants and Animals: by Professor C. E. Bessey, M. S., of the Iowa Agricultural College.

"5. On Stock Breeding: by Professor W. H. Brewer, A. M., Botanist of the California Geological Survey, and Professor of Agriculture in the Sheffield Scientific School.

"6. A miscellaneous course of subjects pertaining to agriculture. The following gentlemen have been invited to lecture:

"On Insects Injurious to Vegetation : Henry Edwards, Esq., San Francisco.

"On Forestry: Professor H. N. Bolander, Sacramento.

"On Orange Culture: Dr. J. Strentzel, Martinez.

"On Wheat: Horace Davis, Esq., San Francisco.

"On Local Field Botany: Dr. W. P. Gibbons, Alameda; Dr. A. Kellogg, San Francisco.

"On Cotton Culture: J. W. A. Wright, M. A.

"On the History of California Agriculture: W. B. Ewer, M. A., San Francisco.

"On the Lower Forms of Vegetable Life: Dr. H. W. Harkness, San Francisco.

"On the Eucalyptus Tree: Mr. R. E. C. Stearns, Berkeley."

COLLEGE OF MECHANICS.

50. Instruction in the science of Mechanics has been given in the University by Professor John Le Conte since 1870, but for the further development of the College of Mechanics, two new instructors have been appointed recently—Professor Hesse and Professor Hoffmann; the former to give instructions in Industrial Mechanics, and the latter in Industrial Drawing. These gentlemen are regarded as qualified in a high degree to give efficiency to this part of the University. Professor Hoffmann's classes are already well organized, and he has begun a collection of diagrams and models which will prove very helpful in his work. An order has been sent to Darmstadt for a collection of Schroeder models illustrative of the elements of mechanism, to be purchased at an outlay of $1,000, and their arrival may be soon expected.

Professor Hesse began his service after the work of the year was so far in progress that it was not easy at the moment to organize a class for his instruction, though he has offered to give special instruction to all who wish it.

In the meantime, he has undertaken to make an investigation which will undoubtedly have a very important bearing upon the industries of this State—an investigation of the strength of the timbers which are grown upon the Pacific Coast. Accurate information is very much needed on this subject by all who are concerned in the use of woods. In order to devise a successful mode of procedure, a meeting was held in February of the present year, which was attended by most of the scientific professors in the University, and by several well-known engineers and builders whose pursuits had caused them to pay particular attention to the character of the woods of this coast. By their united suggestions, a plan was devised for the collection of specimens, and for determining accurately the circumstances of growth. By the agency of the Central Pacific Railroad and Wells, Fargo & Co., these specimens will be collected from every part of the State and brought to Oakland. Meanwhile, Mr. Hesse is engaged in the construction of the instruments by which the woods will be tested. The results of this work will be communicated to the Legislature, and will be published for the benefit of all who are engaged in any department of construction. The suggestions of Professor Bessey, who took a lively interest in this matter, should here be gratefully mentioned.

51. As a preliminary statement of what he has undertaken, Professor Hesse has given me the following note:

OAKLAND, March 22, 1875.

"Having been intrusted with the management of the experimental inquiry relating to the woods of the Pacific slope, I deem it proper, on the eve of your departure for the East, to give you a short synopsis of the progress made so far, and of my views as to its ultimate practical value.

"I am justified in stating, that with the co-operation of the Pacific Railroad Company, Wells, Fargo & Co., and the Scientific Department of the University of California, results can be obtained more comprehensive, and, I hope, more thorough than any yet produced in the East or in Europe. Our slope is noted for the variety and quality of its timber, which has already attracted the attention of the manufacturing interests of Europe, and a knowledge of its properties will not only guide the manufacturer in its selection, but lead to new applications.

"Circulars, containing questions calculated to elicit every possible kind of information, have been printed for the use of the collectors. The specimens, consisting of entire segments of the trunk, will be forwarded to San Francisco to undergo the process of seasoning. This preparatory work will naturally extend over quite a period of time, during which the tests are being made as fast as the specimens can be furnished. The students will assist in the experimental tests, to get accustomed to the handling of instruments for experimental inquiry.

"At present I am engaged in the construction of the necessary apparatus to make the following experiments :

"1. On the strength of direct cohesion of the fibres of wood.
"2. On the lateral adhesion.
"3. On the transverse strength.

"The mechanical action of the strain, which takes place in test 1, is by far the simplest, yet the most difficult to submit to actual experiment in wood.

And it is to some extent owing to this circumstance that so little agreement is found in the experimental results obtained heretofore. For this reason it has been my especial aim in the construction of the apparatus to remove all the objectionable features, which might prevent the obtaining of a reliable result. The main points which claimed my attention in this connection have reference,

"To the influence of vibrations during the test.

"To the necessity of applying the strain in the direct line of the fibres and of the mathematical axis of the body to be tested.

"To adapt the apparatus to the testing of the lateral adhesion of the fibres of the wood.

"I am confident in stating that the plan I have adopted completely covers these points.

"The drawings are now in the hands of the pattern-makers, and I look to the completion of the test machine in a very short time.

"I may mention here, that I attach great importance to test 2, for the following reasons :

"The recognized formula for transverse strength is probably correct only for that material which presents the same cohesive strength in every direction, as is generally found in homogeneous substances. In most woods we find a very different condition. The lateral cohesion is often one-twentieth or less of the direct cohesion of the fibres. The established formula, which measures the resisting force directly by the breadth, the square of the depth, and inversely by the length, is based on theoretic considerations, embracing only direct cohesion and compression, and assumes that lateral cohesion is sufficient to resist the resultant shearing forces. I doubt the correctness of such general assumption, and believe, moreover, that the elasticity of the wood, under the action of forces parallel to the fibres (shearing forces), ought to be separated in the formula.

"I have for this reason consulted the tests that were made by Buffon, under the auspices of the French government, as to the transverse strength of oak of various dimensions, and by far the most valuable ever made, both as respects the number and the size of the pieces of timber on which they were made. Now, if the old formula is correct, the constants computed from each of the above-mentioned experiments ought to approximate the total average result. But I found that these co-efficients decreased rapidly with an increase of the ratio of the depth with the length of beam, which seems practically to bear out the above assertion.

"I am at present engaged in the investigation of the distributed forces, to establish, if possible, that relation above mentioned, and if successful, the results obtained from experiments can be applied so as to produce a more reliable result, a point of great practical utility.

"To Mr. Chauncey Taylor I have to express my thanks for his kindness in offering any facilities which his lumber-yard may afford, and also the results of his experience as to the best selection for my purpose.

. "I must also mention in this connection Joseph Moore, the able Superintendent of the Risdon Iron Works, for having presented me with a steelyard, and for his readiness to assist the enterprise."

52. The following circular has been issued in regard to this investigation.

"The University of California, with the generous co-operation of railroad engineers, and others practically interested in the investigations, proposes to make a thorough examination of the timbers grown and used on the Pacific Coast —especially for the purpose of ascertaining their strength, durability, and adaptation to various industrial, engineering, architectural, mechanical, and manufacturing purposes.

"The result of these investigations will be reported to the Legislature and published for the benefit of the people in this State and at a distance. The suggestions and co-operation of scientific and practical men will be greatly appreciated.

"By the agency of the C. P. R. R. Co., S. P. R. R. Co., and Wells, Fargo & Co., specimens will be collected and brought to the University. The mechanical tests will be made by F. G. Hesse, Oakland, Professor of Industrial Mechanics, and he will be assisted in other departments of the investigation by the professors of Botany, Agriculture, Chemistry, Physics, and Engineering.

"In connection with this work, the collections of the University in Economic Botany and Vegetation will be increased. Interesting specimens for the Museum are solicited. Communications on the subject may be addressed to the Secretary of the University.

"NOTES TO ACCOMPANY EACH SPECIMEN:

"Number.

"Collector's name.

"Date when cut.

"NAME OF TREE: Common and Local. [If several names are known, mention them.] Botanical.

"PLACE WHERE GROWN: State. County. Altitude. [Near summit, or foot of mountain, and on what side.]

"Whether native growth or cultivated.

"Whether isolated or surrounded by other trees of the same kind; if otherwise, state what kind of trees.

"Exposure.

"Nature of soil, moist or dry.

"Knowledge of the durability of wood.

"General condition of the tree, height, age, health, or soundness.

"DIRECTIONS FOR CUTTING.—Cut segments of the trunk five feet long; one, from five to ten feet above ground, according to size of tree; another in middle, and one near top. Collect foliage, branches, and fruit (including acorns, cones, seeds, etc.), to ascertain the botanical name. Mark on each piece the number of the tree (corresponding with the label), the collector's name, and whether cut above ground, at the middle, or top; and also the north point of compass. Include forest trees, acclimated, and second growth."

COLLEGE OF ENGINEERING.

53. The College of Engineering was organized after the appointment of Professor Soulé, in 1871, and has been steadily strengthened from year to year. The services of Mr. Hoffmann are already found to be of great value to the students of this course. The preliminary mathematical studies, which are taught with great thoroughness during the first two years of the University curriculum, give a substantial foundation for the later professional studies of civil, mining, and mechanical engineering. A subdivision of this course, with reference to the profession of the architect, will doubtless, at some future day, be desirable.

This department has an excellent collection of instruments, including transits, levels, barometers, etc., which are constantly used in field work by the students; a superior plane-table and a solar compass have been ordered. It has also the beginning of a collection, made by Professor Soulé, of models of engineering construction, arches, domes, roof and bridge trusses, etc. It has also a valuable cabinet, exhibiting the woods and metals used in construction, artificial stones, cements, preserved woods, etc. Among its maps and diagrams are many of those published by the U. S. Coast Survey, U. S. Lake Survey, U. S. Engineer Corps.

The study of astronomy is aided by globes and astronomical diagrams, by the plates illustrative of the heavenly bodies, published by the Observatory at Cambridge, and by the photographs taken at Mr. Rutherford's Observatory. By the liberality of the War Department, several valuable astronomical instruments have been recently loaned to the University.

COLLEGE OF CHEMISTRY.

54. The College of Chemistry was organized after the return of Professor Rising from Europe, and his commencement of work in the autumn of 1872. The completion of extensive and well arranged laboratories, the appointment of several assistants, and the introduction of practical labor-

atory exercises as a part of the elementary instruction in chemistry of all the University students, and the engagement of a lecturer on metallurgy, are among the measures which have given a rapid development to this college. Its course of studies has been carefully arranged for those who can remain four years; but ample facilities are afforded to all who wish for the opportunity to make for a shorter time a specialty of chemistry.

Professor Rising has furnished me with the following account of the Laboratories for Analytical Chemistry:

"These were planned after the most careful study of the newest and best-arranged laboratories of this country and Europe, with the aid and advice of many experienced teachers of analytical chemistry. They are commodious, convenient, well-lighted, and adapted to the study of analytical chemistry in all its branches and to the carrying on of original research.

"The Qualitative Laboratory, on the first floor, is thirty by fifty feet, with a southern exposure, and is lighted by nine large windows and well ventilated. On the sides of the room are six evaporating niches, closed by glass slides, where acids and the like substances may be evaporated and the fumes entirely excluded from the building. A sand-bath inclosed by a glass hood and provided with a good ventilating flue for evaporations; a muffle for drying, roasting, and igniting substances; and a furnace for fusions, furnish the needed facilities for all chemical operations in the laboratory which require direct heat.

"The room contains eight working-tables, each table intended for four students, thus accommodating thirty-two. These tables are nearly an exact copy of those in the University Laboratory at Berlin, and are very complete and convenient. Each student is supplied with water and sink, etc., and has a complete set of re-agents under his control. The tables are also provided with gas connections, and gas will soon be supplied to the laboratory.

"A small room intended for a sulphureted-hydrogen room, and provided with hood, tables, sink, etc., connects with this main room.

"Another room, also connecting with the main laboratory, is intended for a re-agent and apparatus room, but is temporarily used as a laboratory for elementary chemistry.

"Adjoining the sulphureted-hydrogen room, but not connected with it, is a room designed for gas analysis.

"Another room on the same floor was designed for toxicology, but is now used for another purpose.

"On the second floor, immediately above the Qualitative Laboratory, is the Quantitative Laboratory, also thirty by fifty feet, with very high ceilings and well-lighted. This room, like the one below, is provided with evaporating niches and eight students' desks of black walnut, and accommodates the same number of students (thirty-two). A sand and steam-bath, with hood

and drying ovens, supplies the needed accommodations for evaporation, drying precipitates, etc.; also, all the distilled water needed in the laboratories.
A number of Bunsen's filter pumps supplies an abundant opportunity for
rapid filtration. Glass cases on either side of the main entrance to the
Quantitative Laboratory are intended to contain a chemical cabinet. Here
are to be placed collections of chemical compounds neatly put up and labeled
and systematically arranged. They are placed where they must be almost
constantly seen by the students, and are intended for instruction. The ven-
tilation of this room is also good.

"Connecting with this room is a fusion and re-agent room. This room
contains a blast lamp, conveniences for organic analysis, a hood with ventilating flue, shelves and cases for re-agents, etc.

"Convenient to the main laboratory is a balance room, supplied with
three of Becker's best balances. This number will be increased as the needs
of the department demand. The room also contains a few scales for rougher
weighing.

"A private laboratory for the Professor of Chemistry connects with the
Quantitative Laboratory. This is of moderate size, and is supplied with two
working-tables like those in the main room, but smaller. It also contains a table
with pneumatic cistern, sink, cupboard, cases, shelves, drawers, etc. Here the
finer apparatus, glass-ware, etc., to be used in research, is stored.

"LABORATORY FOR ELEMENTARY CHEMISTRY.—This. laboratory was not
provided for in the original plan. The most available room for the purpose
was the apparatus room of the Qualitative Laboratory, and this room is used
for that purpose until a better place can be provided. It is very plainly fitted
up with shelves, tables, cases, and cupboards, and accommodates at one time
twelve students.

"All the students of the University, at some time during their course, must
complete a course of practical chemistry in the laboratory. The rapidly increasing number of students in the University will soon make it necessary
to provide a larger and more convenient room for this purpose.

"CHEMICAL LECTURE-ROOM.—The room immediately above the Quantitative Laboratory was designed for a chemical lecture - room. It is provided with a long lecture-table, at one end of which is a sink and pneumatic
cistern. Underneath the sink and cistern are two gasometers, which are to
supply oxygen and hydrogen when wanted during the lecture. At the end of
the table is a mercury cistern, a flue for carrying off noxious gases, etc. Back
of the table are two evaporating niches, a blackboard, etc., and on either
side cases for chemicals and apparatus needed for illustration of lectures. A
small hoist connects with the laboratory below.

"The seats are arranged in rows, one above the other, so that the view of
the lecture-table is never obstructed.

"The room itself is exceedingly pleasant; it is thirty by fifty feet, twenty-
three feet high, and lighted with a large skylight covered with ground glass,
and four large windows.

"CHEMICAL APPARATUS FOR THE USE OF STUDENTS.—The Laboratories for
Elementary and Analytical Chemistry are supplied with the apparatus needed
in the prosecution of the study of these branches. This is loaned to the

students, and may be returned to the Laboratory without charge if not damaged.

"The Laboratory has two spectroscopes for the use of students, and when gas is supplied every student of chemistry will have an opportunity of becoming practically acquainted with their use.

"The Laboratory has a good supply of such apparatus as may be needed in carrying on original investigations.

"CHEMICAL APPARATUS FOR ILLUSTRATING LECTURES.—This includes a set of Hoffmann's apparatus for illustrating volumetric composition, made by Geisler at Berlin, a Bunsen battery, induction coil, glass-ware, crystal models, collections of minerals, diagrams, etc. A set of furnace models, manufactured by Schuhmann of Freiberg, is soon to arrive.

"The total cost of chemical apparatus, including that for the use of students and for illustrating lectures, was about $8,000."

COLLEGE OF MINES.

55. This department has recently been organized under the direction of Professor Ashburner, and its plans will be developed as fast as the funds are provided. During the coming year, Dr. Becker will instruct in Metallurgy, and Professor Hilgard will form a class in Mineralogy, and this will be in addition to the instructions given as heretofore by the Professors Le Conte, Rising, and others.

The geological and mineralogical collections of the University are very extensive, and are now being arranged, as elsewhere stated, by Mr. H. G. Hanks.

LECTURES ON THE USEFUL ARTS.

56. In connection with the Colleges of Mining, Mechanics, Engineering, and Chemistry, arrangements were made during the session of 1874-5, for the delivery at Berkeley of various special lectures upon subjects relating to useful arts. These lectures are in addition to the systematic and prolonged instruction given to the classes by the professors in Geology, Physics, Mechanics, Chemistry, Engineering, and other branches of study. Special lectures are open to all who wish to attend them, whether members of the University or not.

"1. A course of Lectures on the Useful Metals; by Dr. George F. Becker graduate of the Royal School of Mines, Berlin.

"Subjects discussed—Metallurgy as a Science; Fuel, Refractory Material, and Furnaces; Lead; Copper; Mercury; Silver; Gold; Zinc; Iron."

4

Single lectures on the following subjects:

"2. On Mining as a Profession: by William Ashburner, Professor of Mining, University of California.

"3. On the Science of Mechanics: by Frederick G. Hesse. Professor of Mechanics, University of California.

"4. On Industrial or Mechanical Drawing: by John D. Hoffmann, Instructor in Industrial Drawing, University of California.

"5. On the Proposed Improvement of Oakland Harbor (San Leandro Creek): by Julian Le Conte, C. E., Oakland.

"6. On the Geodetic Survey of Colorado, under Dr. Hayden: by A. D. Wilson, and F. Rhoda, Officers of the U. S. Geological Survey of the Territories, Washington, D. C.

"7. On the Present State of the Art of Telegraphy: by James Gamble, and S. D. Field, of the Western Union Telegraph Company, San Francisco.

"8. On Electro-metallurgy: by Dr. A. Kellogg, San Francisco.

"9. On the Timbers in Common Use: by Professor C. E. Bessey, of the Iowa College of Agriculture.

"10. On the Preservation of Woods: by I. C. Woods, of the Wood Preserving Works, San Francisco.

"11. On Coal as a Raw Material: by Professor W. H. Brewer, of the Sheffield Scientific School, Yale College."

57. While prominence is given to technical and scientific instruction, the University of California is so organized that literary, historical, and philosophical studies are not neglected. The Regents have been impartial in their plans for the development of all departments of the University, fully recognizing the responsibility which the law places upon them to maintain a " College of Letters " as well as " Colleges of Science." All scientific students connected with the University are expected to devote a part of their attention to literary subjects, just as all the literary students receive instruction in the natural sciences. Important as technical instruction may be, the State of California can not afford to neglect the study of man; and its University would be unworthy of the name of university, if ample provision were not made for the study of language, literature, morals, history, and art, or if the methods of accumulating material wealth were represented to her youth, in the highest educational institution of the Pacific Coast, as more important than the methods of forming character and promoting culture.

COLLEGE OF LETTERS.

58. The College of Letters now offers two courses of instruction, one of which is chiefly based upon Ancient Languages and Literature; the other, upon Modern. The former is called the Classical Course; the other, the Literary. The Classical Course needs no explanation here. It corresponds with that of other classical colleges, and leads to the degree of Bachelor of Arts. The Literary Course is quite new in our University. It corresponds during the first two years with the scientific courses above enumerated, and during the last two years provides a liberal training in modern languages, history, and literature, and in those departments of science taught in the University which are of the most general interest. It leads to the degree of Bachelor of Philosophy.

59. Special prominence has always been given in this institution to the study of the continental languages of Europe. In this department there is now a professor, qualified to teach French, German, Spanish, and Italian; and there are three special instructors in addition—one in French, one in German, and one in Spanish. Every student who takes a degree is expected to be familiar with French and German, and he may at his option pursue also the study of Spanish and Italian. Special students are received in these studies.

60. In the Classical department or college the Professor of Ancient Languages, Mr. Kellogg, has commenced the delivery of extended courses of lectures on Ancient Literature and Archæology, in the illustration of which he is greatly assisted by the photographs, diagrams, maps, and coins, which have been presented to the institution chiefly by Mr. C. W. Howard. The pronunciation of Latin according to what is called "the continental method" is now taught.

For the most fruitful conduct of this department (steadily increasing in numbers), it seems important that still more time be given to courses of lectures. These condense the results of much study, and bring before the students connected views of ancient life, literature, politics, and philosophy; topics which deeply interest the student of the ancient world, and have important bearings on the literature, the thought, the government, and the political life of modern times.

The Senior Instructor in this department should have time for courses of lectures—longer or shorter—to each of the four classes, in each half of the academic year, viz:

To the Freshmen—On Ancient Geography; on the Classical Side of English.

To the Juniors—On Greek and Roman Mythology; on Greek and Roman Archæology.

To the Sophomores—On the Latin Authors; on the Greek Authors.

To the Seniors—On Greek and Roman Literature; on Greek and Roman Politics; on Greek and Roman Philosophy; on Linguistics.

Three or four of these courses are already in progress. But to carry out the whole plan, involving more than one hundred carefully prepared lectures each year, which must be freshened and renewed continually by the latest investigations and authorities, the lecturer must be relieved from a larger share of text-book recitations. He now has eight recitations a week, besides three courses of lectures.

This is only one of many ways in which the instruction in this department may be made wider and more effective. The class-room drill is all-important, and will soon demand the subdivision of each class. One of the Latin classes has this year been reciting in two sections; one of the Greek classes so recited last year.

61. In respect to the Literary course, the following notes have been made by one of the chief instructors in it (Professor Sill):

. "The Literary course, inaugurated at the beginning of this year, has proved already very attractive. Of the Junior class sixteen are pursuing this course, including special students, making nearly a quarter of the regular class in this one of the seven courses open to them.

"In the Sophomore class it is impossible to tell how many will enter as Literary students, since their choice is not manifested till next year; but from the number who are availing themselves of the opportunity to make up their deficiency in Latin (which is required for this course), and from other indications, it is believed that they will number more than the preceding class.

"Of the Freshman class there is reason to expect a still larger portion will choose the Literary course.

"The attractiveness of this line of studies newly opened to them is indicated by the fact that of the whole number of special students, one-half are enrolled in the Literary course.

"Some idea of its scope may be gained from the work of the present term.

"The Junior class is midway in March's 'Comparative Grammar of the Anglo-Saxon and Kindred Languages,' and is just commencing to read the Anglo-Saxon Gospel in Corson's 'Handbook of Anglo-Saxon and Early English.' They have besides a weekly exercise in Literary History and Biography, calling for written results of special investigations of their own. Each week, also, they prepare and read an essay in some special style of literary effort.

"The Sophomore and Freshman classes, as the schedule is at present constituted, all have the same studies (except the classical students), whatever course they may be expecting to choose in Junior year. Of these various studies, much less time is given to those which look toward English culture, and the Literary course in particular, than toward the courses of Natural Science, etc. This is unfortunate; especially as their preparatory training is much less satisfactory on this side than on the side of Mathematics and Classics. The Sophomore class are just finishing Whateley's 'Rhetoric.' They have weekly an exercise in writing and reading essays in different branches of composition.

"The Freshman class are about finishing Hadley's 'Brief History of the English Language.' They also have a weekly composition exercise.

"The entire Junior class, as well as those in the Literary course proper, are studying Taine's 'History of English Literature.'

"The whole Senior class have a weekly exercise in literary study, with essays.

"It may be noted as an encouraging sign for this side of culture, that the students show a genuine appetite for whatever English or literary advantages are opened to them. Our Library is visited all day long by groups of quiet, earnest workers, whose faces as well as their persistent diligence show their appreciation of what has been done for them in that direction. The composition classes, too, besides plenty of chance indications constantly showing themselves here and there, speak of the growing presence of that spirit of literary and intellectual force and refinement, which the world over makes the English 'gentleman and scholar.'

"What we need in the English studies is a larger share of time, in the conduct of studies; better preparatory training, as the first way of saving time, and more books in both the Reference and Circulating Libraries."

62. Arrangements have been made during the session of 1874–5, for the delivery at Berkeley of various special lectures upon historical and literary subjects, in addition to the systematic instruction given to the classes by the pro-

fessors and instructors. Special lectures are open to all who wish to attend them, whether members of the University or not.

Among others, the following lectures have been announced:

"1. On the study of Modern Languages: by P. Pioda, Professor of Modern Languages.

"2. On the study of English: by E. R. Sill, Professor of English.

"3. On the study of Spanish: by C. F. Gompertz, Instructor in Spanish.

"4. On Schiller's 'Song of the Bell:' by A. Putzker, Instructor in German.

"5. On the Crimean War (in French): by G. De Kersaint-Gily, Instructor in French.

"6. On Scottish Poetry: by Hon. H. H. Haight, San Francisco.

"7. On a subject to be announced: by Rev. H. Stebbins, D. D., San Francisco.

"8. On a subject to be announced: by Hon. S. H. Phillips, San Francisco.

"9. On the Literary and Scientific Progress of California during twenty-five years (1849–74): by William C. Bartlett, Esq., San Francisco.

"10. On Gesture Language: by Prof. Wilkinson, Principal of the California Institution for the Deaf, Dumb, and Blind, Berkeley.

"11. On the History of Explorations of the Rocky Mountains: by W. H. Brewer, Professor in Yale College.

"12. A Course of Lectures on Constitutional Law: by Hon. Stephen J. Field, one of the Justices of the U. S. Supreme Court, Professor of Law in the University of California."

MEDICAL COLLEGE.

63. On the fourth of March, 1873, a communication was received by the Regents, from the Trustees of the Toland Medical College, proposing to convey all the property of that institution to the University of California. The gift included land, building, and apparatus, and was made in the name of the original donor, Dr. H. H. Toland.

This unconditional gift was accepted by the Regents, who were thus brought, at once, to the consideration of organizing a medical department. An effort was made to unite the two medical faculties then existing in San Francisco, but it was not successful. As a preliminary arrangement most of the medical gentlemen who had been connected with the Toland College, together with several gentlemen appointed by the Regents from other parts of the State, consented to carry forward the usual courses of instruction, without any other compensation than that which might be received from fees.

64. In order to determine upon a plan for the organization of this department on a permanent and satisfactory basis, the Regents requested a large committee of medical men to consider and report such suggestions as seemed to them wise. Two reports were received from this committee, but neither one seemed to the Regents entirely satisfactory. Both left the medical department behind the other departments of the University, in its standard of requirements for admission, when it should be decidedly in advance. These reports were received and laid upon the table. Several of the professors have since resigned, and the question of the future has been referred to the Advisory Committee to consider and report upon. Two courses of lectures have been given and two classes have been graduated under the authority of the Regents.

ORIENTAL COLLEGE.

65. By the terms of a gift of Mr. Tompkins, the Regents have come under obligations to establish and maintain a professorship of Oriental Languages, especially of Chinese and Japanese. Letters have already been exchanged with an eminent scholar in Chinese, with reference to his acceptance of this chair.

66. At the opening of Congress in December, 1873, President Grant recommended that the Japanese Indemnity Fund be devoted to educational purposes. Subsequently, the following bill was brought before the United States Senate, by Hon. A. A. Sargent, and referred to the Committee on Foreign Relations. Its purport is, to bestow annually the income which shall be derived from the "Japanese Indemnity Fund" upon a board of seven trustees. These trustees are to maintain, in connection with the University

of California, "au Oriental College," which will have three objects: 1. To promote international acquaintance and good-will, by assembling a body of learned teachers who shall inquire into and make known the languages, laws, religions, and political institutions of the Orient; 2. To afford young Americans an opportunity to fit themselves for diplomatic, consular, mercantile, and scientific careers in Asia; and 3. To give to young Japanese an opportunity to become acquainted with the civilization of the western nations.

"A BILL MAKING PROVISION FOR AN ORIENTAL COLLEGE.—*Be it enacted*, etc., That the Secretary of the Treasury is hereby authorized and directed to invest the proceeds of the Indemnity Fund paid by the government of Japan to the government of the United States, under the convention of Simonoseki of October 22, 1864, now remaining in the Treasury, in five per centum gold-bearing bonds of the United States, and to annually pay the income thereof to seven trustees, to be appointed by the President of the United States, for the uses hereinafter mentioned.

"SEC. 2. That the President of the United States shall appoint, by and with the advice and consent of the Senate, a board of seven trustees, to serve without pay, and from time to time, as vacancies occur in said board, shall fill such vacancies; which said trustees shall maintain, in connection with the University of California, and with such other institutions of learning as may seem likely to promote the purposes of this endowment, an Oriental College, the object of which shall be to promote a knowledge of the languages, history, religions, laws, manners, resources, and commercial relations of Asiatic countries, for the sake of increasing international friendship and intercourse; and also to afford American youths an opportunity to fit themselves for residence and service in the Orient, as diplomatic or consular agents and interpreters, or for private careers; and also to afford Japanese youths an opportunity to pursue their education in this country under favorable circumstances.

"SEC. 3. That said trustees shall annually, upon meeting of Congress, report to the President of the United States the financial and educational condition of their trust."

The *Overland Monthly* said, in respect to this proposition:

"It is obvious that if such a college is to be established in this country there are many reasons why it should be placed in the neighborhood of San Francisco. Through this harbor, in all time to come, intercourse will be maintained between the United States and Asiatic countries. Here it is that young Chinese and Japanese students first arrive; here are already liberal opportunities for them to acquire a knowledge of the sciences and arts of our western culture. The University of California, from the time of its opening, has stood open to students from any State or country, free from all charges for tuition. The climate of the Pacific Coast is more favorable than that of the Atlantic for those who come from the Orient. A knowledge of Japan and the other countries of Asia is especially important to the people of California, who, partly by necessity and partly by preference, must always maintain close relations with the countries upon the opposite shores of the Pacific."

MANUAL LABOR AND PECUNIARY ASSISTANCE.

67. One of the best characteristics of the American colleges is the bringing together, on terms of equality, free from artificial and conventional distinctions, young men of different pecuniary conditions. The sons of the rich and of the needy grow up side by side, and the honors which they receive from one another and from the faculty are bestowed without any reference to the homes from which they come. Thus year after year many of the highest distinctions are bestowed upon those whose struggles for an education have been carried on in the face of extreme poverty and sometimes of other great embarrassments. In the University of California, as in other kindred institutions, the honors of literary and scientific distinction are thus bestowed upon the most meritorious, without any reference to their antecedent training. It is a great advantage of a system of public education, particularly in this country, that it brings together on terms of complete scholastic equality those whose material circumstances differ so widely. Almost every college of the country has found it expedient in some way or other to provide suitable encouragement to young persons while pursuing their courses of study. During four years of the history of the University of California, there were five scholarships the incumbents of which received each an income of three hundred dollars per year, from the beginning to the end of their course, and some of the most meritorious scholars here graduated owe their education to this timely assistance; but the change in the law effected by the Political Code abolished these scholarships, and no such aid is now given.

68. The authorities of the University, however, have

done all in their power to throw into the hands of those who wished it opportunities to earn money in various ways. Some students have given private instruction to other students who needed assistance in their studies; others have been employed on holidays and in vacations and in their leisure hours in rendering assistance in various manual occupations, both in work upon the grounds and elsewhere; some have taken care of the buildings, and some of the heating apparatus.

69. Another agency by which many have found it convenient to add to their income has been employment in the Printing-office. The Printing-office was commenced soon after the University was removed to Berkeley, by the purchase of type and a press at a cost of $1,350, which was given to the University by one of the Regents. Subsequently, the Regents appropriated the sum of $2,500 for the purpose of expanding this office. It has been found an exceedingly convenient part of the apparatus at Berkeley, and has been the means also of imparting to many of the students a knowledge of a useful art and of enabling many deserving persons to add considerably to their income. So far as students have desired work in connection with the farm and garden they have been allowed the opportunity, and in this, as in all other cases, have been paid the usual wages for their labor. At the same time it should never be forgotten that the scholastic duties of the various courses of instruction are so severe as to task all the powers of the young men who are here studying, and to diminish their capacity for manual labor. The ability to add to one's income by hard work while pursuing a course of study varies very much with individuals. Some are able to do a great deal in this way without impairing their standing as scholars; but, as a general rule, it is obvious that the chief business of every student should be the mastery of his lessons.

A Students' Loan Association has been organized by a number of liberal gentlemen, though as yet no funds have

been paid in. To this association we may look with con-
fidence for aid in the future to deserving students.

INSTRUCTION OF YOUNG WOMEN.

70. When the University of California was organized its
doors were freely opened to all properly qualified students
above a certain age. Young ladies were admitted as well
as young men, and the invitation was freely extended to
students from any country and from any State, without reference to their race or condition, to avail themselves of the
advantages here freely bestowed. The number of young
ladies who have been taught in the institution from its
foundation has been as follows: in 1870–71, 8; 1871–72, 27;
1872–73, 39; 1873–74, 22; 1874–75, 39. One of these has
graduated; twelve are now members of regular courses of
instruction, as candidates for degrees. But by far the
larger number of these young ladies have been attendants
upon special courses of instruction, especially upon the
lessons of the professors of modern languages. The scholar-
ship of those who have entered the regular courses of instruction has for the most part been excellent, and in some
cases has been of the very highest rank. Among the
regular students the proportion of ladies who have been
good scholars has been greater than that of young men.

THE LIBRARY.

71. The general reference library of the University is now
placed on the main floor of the south hall. This is regarded
as only a temporary arrangement until a proper building
can be constructed. The reason for the selection of this
room was its accessibility, its light and cheerful character,
and the fire-proof construction of the building. The library
is arranged by subjects in alcoves and in cases, which are
handsomely made with reference to their removal in the
right time to a new building. The library remains quite
small, but is an excellent nucleus for a college library,
especially in English and French books. There are but

few in other languages. The nucleus of the library is derived from an appropriation by the Regents, of $5,000,, made several years ago, and expended chiefly under the direction of the Library Committee. To this have been added numerous generous gifts from individuals, the most noteworthy of which are the following: A collection of cyclopedias, and other works of reference, from Mr. E. L. Goold; the literary and art books, with some scientific treatises, which belonged to the late Mr. Pioche, and which are for the most part, very handsomely bound; the library of Dr. Lieber (which was particularly full in works pertaining to political and social science, and included many rare tracts and pamphlets), the gift of Michael Reese; and the professional library of the late Dr. Fourgeaud, consisting of several hundred volumes, well-bound, of medical works in French and English. The legislature of the State, in 1873, made a special appropriation of the sum of $4,800 for the increase of the library, and with this amount large accessions are about to be made. The number of volumes is about 12,000, or more than double what it was in 1872.

72. It is intended that the main library of the University shall be chiefly a reference library, so that scholars in any department may be sure of finding upon the shelves the various treatises which they wish to consult; consequently permission to draw books from this library is given only in exceptional cases. But in building up the reference library it is necessary to keep in mind also the need of supplying the students with books which they can take to their rooms with freedom; and consequently a branch circulating library has been begun in the north hall. This circulating library is made up, in part, from the duplicate books belonging to the main library, and in part from the gifts of individuals, among whom the members of the senior class of 1875 are particularly entitled to recognition. Two other branch libraries have also been begun. The best and most important books pertaining to the science of agriculture

have been transferred to the lecture-room of the Professor of Agriculture, and some of those pertaining to the useful arts will be in a like manner made accessible to professors and teachers in the rooms devoted to instruction in Mechanics. The gift of Mr. Pioche, and the gifts of other individuals, have made it possible to begin also a group of books relating particularly to the fine arts. In due time it is hoped that every one of the chief rooms of instruction will be furnished with the books which pertain to the studies there pursued. Thus the rooms devoted to modern languages should be supplied with the best dictionaries, grammars, and standard literary works. There should be a reference mathematical library within easy reach of the instructors of Mathematics. And so in Engineering, in Chemistry, in historical and political subjects, the books most constantly needed by professors or students should be within easy reach. Thus the main library would be to the University a general store-house, a place of resort for the professors and students when they wished to prosecute their studies, while the instruments needed for daily service would be kept within easy reach, in the ordinary places of study and instruction. It is proposed that the room commonly called the Young Men's Reading-room, or Club-room, on the lower floor of the north hall, be supplied with the current magazines and newspapers, and made accessible at all hours of the day. It would be a great advantage to the University if some one of the library rooms could be lighted and opened by night, in order thus to encourage the use of books in the leisure hours which are at command of the various students. Bancroft Library

73. In speaking of the library, special attention should be called to the fact that a very large collection has been made of newspapers illustrative of the history of California. Among the extended sets which have been given by various individuals, the following are noteworthy: the *New York Times*, the *Sacramento Union*, the *San Francisco Chronicle*, first series, the *San Francisco Bulletin*, the *Alta California*,

and the *Herald*. It is very desirable that as the library grows this department should be steadily increased, and in other ways the effort should be put forth to bring together everything in the way of books, pamphlets, periodicals, and newspapers, which may throw light upon the history of the Pacific Coast.

STUDENTS' LODGING-HOUSES.

74. Upon the removal of the University to Berkeley, the Regents at first determined to do nothing toward the establishment of lodging - houses for the scholars, but to depend entirely upon private persons to supply the requisite homes. They caused advertisements to be inserted in the newspapers, and announcements to be otherwise publicly made to this effect, but after months of delay it became evident that private individuals would do but little for the supply of homes. Efforts were made to form associations for the purpose of providing homes or halls in the neighborhood of the University; but these efforts have not yet succeeded.

75. The Regents were therefore compelled to construct a few houses upon their own grounds, and at their own expense, for the use of students. Eight cottages, each of them adapted to ten students, were accordingly constructed upon a convenient plan and of tasteful appearance. Volunteer clubs were formed among the students to hire these cottages, at a rental of $300 per annum, or $30 per month during the year of instruction. Each cottage contains five rooms of large size (each designed to be occupied by two persons), a dining-room, a kitchen, and a servant's room; a bath-room, with other needed conveniences, was also constructed.

These cottages were rented by the University to the clubs, without any agency on the part of the Faculty. Good order was required from those who occupied them, but no attempt was made on the part of the authorities to control the internal management of any of these establishments. The relation between the University and the club was

simply that of landlord and tenant, the landlord claiming
the right to eject the tenant for any misdemeanor. It is
too soon to tell how well this system will work. It was a
temporary device in an emergency, and was based upon the
experience of two clubs which had already found abodes in
cottages at Berkeley. Thus far the plan works well.

76. One of the greatest difficulties in the management of
the University arises from the fact that so many of the professors and instructors are non-resident. Such a college
should be surrounded by the homes of those who are engaged in the instruction of the youth; for as soon as a good
neighborhood is formed, other families of culture and of influence may be expected to come to it, and all the attrac-
tions of a college village may be secured. But at present the
neighborhood of Berkeley grows but slowly. There is in
it no school, no practicing physician, and but few and indif-
ferent stores. The walks and roads are in a bad condition
most of the year, and the inconveniences of family life are
great. Families hesitate to remove to Berkeley until they
see that the professors and others who are most interested
in the work which is there going forward, have became residents of the University neighborhood. The law requires
the Secretary to live at Berkeley, and he removed there
soon after accepting the office. Three of the Professors have
built houses for themselves; two occupy cottages belonging to the University, paying rent for them; one has hired
a cottage in the neighborhood, and several of the young-
er instructors have been allowed to occupy small rooms in
the public buildings; but this is all. It seems to me of the
first importance that measures should be taken to provide
homes at Berkeley for all the permanent staff of instructors.
I do not pretend to suggest the best mode of accomplishing
this result, nor the best positions to be set apart for such
houses, but the subject is worthy of the earnest and imme-
diate consideration of the Regents. Prior to the removal

to Berkeley, the authorities had decided to construct a number of houses for the accommodation of the professors; the plans were drawn, and the estimates received, but it appeared to some members of the Board that the Regents had not the necessary authority to take this step, and accordingly the proposed action was reconsidered, and the plan abandoned.

PUBLIC LECTURES.

77. Since the organization of the University, special efforts have been put forth by the authorities to awaken an interest in the work of the University, by means of public lectures upon scientific subjects. In addition to the voluntary work of the various professors, who have been called upon from time to time to go to the different towns in the State, one of the professors, the Professor of Agriculture, was instructed by the Regents to go about the State, and deliver lectures on the subjects to which he was specially devoted; and for six successive years a course of public lectures has been given every winter in San Francisco, at the rooms of the Mechanics' Institute, by various members of the Faculty.

78. An assembly of the students of all departments is held on every Friday afternoon—at which announcements and instructions of general interest are communicated. The various professors and instructors in their turn have given lectures on these occasions, and not infrequently gentlemen who are not connected with the University have been invited to lecture. This appointment has been found quite acceptable to the friends of the University and of the students, who avail themselves of this opportunity to visit Berkeley.

Among the speakers not connected with the Faculty who have addressed the students on these occasions may be mentioned the following:

Hon. Newton Booth, Hon. F. F. Low (late U. S. Minister in China), Rev. Charles Kingsley (Canon of Westminster), President Miner (of Tufts College), Rev. Dr. G. B. Bacon, Dr. W. P. Gibbons, Professor W. Wilkinson, Horace Davis, Esq., Professor Bessey (of Ames, Iowa), Professor Brewer (of New Haven), Dr. G. F. Becker, and Rev. Dr. Stebbins. Several other gentlemen have promised to speak.

79. It should be borne distinctly in mind that it is not supposed these lectures will in any way supersede the systematic instruction which is given by the permanent professors, nor that they are as useful to the students as the instruction of their ordinary and regular teachers; but that while the staff of the University is so small, it is an advantage to strengthen it by calling in from time to time gentlemen who have been interested in various specialties.

FINANCES.

80. Although the administration of finances of the University has not come under my official supervision, it may add to the completeness of this report if I submit some figures derived from the books of the Secretary, and the recent report of the Finance Committee. From this it appears that the total disbursements of the University during the year ending October 31st, 1874, were $95,707.81, of which amount the sum of $64,094.96 was paid in salaries. The other large items of expense were for the development of the agricultural grounds, $5,784.13; insurance, $3,510.65; interest on Brayton property, $4,875.02. The income during the same period was derived from the following sources: From the invested funds, $33,150; from the annual appropriation of the State, $25,193.80; and from land interest, $19,560.03.

During the current two years—1873--75—the appropriation of the Legislature is as follows: For current expenses, $50,000; for the development of the Departments of Agriculture and Mechanic Arts, $30,000; for the Library, $4,800; total, $84,800. For further particulars in this connection, attention is called to the forthcoming annual report of the Secretary.

81. In comparing the receipts of the University of California from the various legislative appropriations, since its foundation, with the receipts of other similar institutions, it will appear that the State has been exceedingly liberal toward this institution, and has enabled it quickly to take a place of influence and power, not only within the limits of the State, but among the various kindred institutions of the country. Everything has been projected upon a large scale, making it necessary that there should be large annual outlays to keep up that which has been so liberally begun. The distance of the University from a large town; the ample grounds which must be brought into cultivation; the laying out and grading of roads and paths; the heating, the repairs, and the daily care of spacious edifices; the incidental supplies of laboratory material, stationery, etc., all involve very large expenditures, and these expenditures must necessarily increase as the years roll on. So again, the number of departments in which instruction is given requires a very large staff of teachers, and this staff must be augmented as the number of scholars increases. As no charges are made for tuition, there will be no increase of income from student fees, which is one of the sources of revenue in other colleges, and as the University is at present organized there can be but little hope of large private gifts for the endowment of the University. It is, therefore, to the Legislature of the State that the authorities must look for the maintenance of the enterprise which has been inaugurated at Berkeley.

AGRICULTURAL LAND.

82. The Committee on Education and Labor of the House of Representatives in Washington, through the Chairman, Mr. Monroe, submitted to Congress on the 13th day of January, 1875, a report on the condition and management of colleges in the various States which had received a grant from the United States under the Act of July 2d, 1862. This report exhibits the amount of money received in every

State from the aforesaid grant, and it shows how success-fully the affairs of the University of California have been managed in comparison with those of other kindred insti-tutions.

It appears that the institutions formed in the various States have received the following prices per acre for the lands which they have sold:

Alabama	$0.90	Missouri	$1.84
Arkansas	.90	Nebraska	—
California	5.00	Nevada	—
Connecticut	.75	New Hampshire	.535
Delaware	.92	New Jersey	.55
Florida	—	New York	.61
Georgia	.90	North Carolina	.50
Illinois	.70	Ohio	.5436
Indiana	.544	Oregon	—
Iowa	2.27	Pennsylvania	.563
Kansas	—	Rhode Island	.415
Kentucky	.50	South Carolina	.725
Louisiana	.87	Tennessee	.90⅝
Maine	.555	Texas	.87
Maryland	.5357	Vermont	.818
Massachusetts	.656	Virginia	.95
Michigan	3.25	West Virginia	.60
Minnesota	5.62	Wisconsin	1.25
Mississippi	.90		

POSSIBLE DEVELOPMENT OF THE UNIVERSITY.

83. The following scheme is here printed to show the re-lations which might easily be established between the Uni-versity and kindred establishments in its vicinity:

A.—STATE COLLEGES AT BERKELEY.

1. The Modern Sciences.—Faculty of Science. Subdivisions.—A select course of Mathematics, Physics, Mechanics, Geology, Zoology, etc.; special courses in the following departments: Agriculture, Chemistry, Civil Engi-neering, Mechanical Engineering, Mining, and Metallurgy.

2. The Liberal Arts.—Faculty of Letters. Subdivisions.—Ancient (Clas-sical Course); Modern (Literary Course); Oriental.

B.—COLLEGES ENDOWED OR SUSTAINED BY THE GENEROSITY OF INDIVIDUALS AT SAN FRANCISCO.

3. The Useful Arts.—Faculty of Industry. (In connection with the Me-chanics' Institute as an affiliated institution). The sum of $15,000 to be ex-

pended annually for two years was subscribed by a few individuals to inaugurate a school of Mechanic Arts; but the proposal of Mr. James Lick to found a Polytechnic School prevented the carrying forward of the plan.

4. The Fine Arts.—Faculty of Art. (In connection with the Art Association of San Francisco as an affiliated institution). A School of Design is already begun.

5. Professional Schools.—Faculty of Medicine. (By the gift of Dr. H. H. Toland, a Medical College building has been provided.) As affiliated institutions: The California College of Pharmacy (in progress); The California College of Dentistry (proposed).

6. Faculty of Law. To be organized.

C.—ADVANCED SCIENTIFIC FOUNDATIONS.

7. The California Academy of Sciences.
8. The Microscopical Society of San Francisco.
9. The Astronomical Observatory.

Respectfully submitted to the Board of Regents.

DANIEL C. GILMAN, President.

www.ingramcontent.com/pod-product-compliance
Lightning Source LLC
Chambersburg PA
CBHW031803090426

42739CB00008B/1135